Free and Hanseatic City of

BREMEN

including Bremerhaven and Worpswede

An illustrated guide to the historical city centre and surrounding area

S0-BAX-366

Text: Wolfgang Kootz

Photos: Jürgen Nogai

Published by Kraichgau Verlag, Dielheim, Germany

History of the City

782   First documentary reference: the heathen tribes of Bremen are in revolt against the rule of Charlemagne and his missionaries. The priest Gerval and his followers are defeated.

787   The priest Willenbad becomes the first bishop of the Lower Weser region and starts building a wooden church, to be dedicated to St Peter.

845   After the Vikings destroy Hamburg, Archbishop Ansgar moves his See to Bremen.

888   The Archbishopric of Bremen is granted market rights.

965   Full market privileges, including the right to mint coins and hold a court of law, granted by the Emperor Otto the Great.

ca. 1000 Bremen ships trade with Nordic countries, England, France, and Spain.

1041   Construction work starts on the present-day cathedral

1043 onwards: Archbishop Adalbert pursues missionary work vigorously. Bremen is called the „Rome of the North".

1234   Battle of Altenesch: Archbishop Gerhard II subjugates the free peasantry on the left bank of the Weser.

1244   A bridge leads across the Weser.

1358   Bremen enters the Hansa trading league, the city having been in possession of Hanseatic privileges since before 1300.

ca. 1400 The Hanseatic city thrives and prospers.

1404   The Statue of Roland is erected, symbolising civil liberties. The archbishop thereupon moves his residence to Bremervörde.

1405-10 Gothic town hall is built.

1522   Reformation in Bremen.

1530   Entry into the Schmalkald League of evangelical princes and Imperial cities.

ca. 1600 Renewed prosperity: the „Schütting" is built, the town hall reconstructed, and the city fortifications enlarged.

1619-22 As the Weser silts up further, a port is built in Vegesack, as one of the first artificial harbours in Germany.

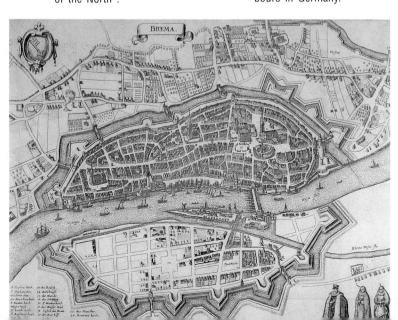

1623	The Counts of Oldenburg impose the Weser Toll for sea trade (it lasts until 1820). End of Hansa agreement.
1646	Bremen becomes a Free Imperial City.
1776	Declaration of Independence by the United States of America. Start of trade with North America, followed shortly after by South America.
1803	Parks and gardens take the place of the city's fortifications.
1806	Bremen becomes a sovereign republic and takes the name of Free Hanseatic City.
1810-13	Bremen is briefly part of the French Empire under Napoleon.
1820 onwards:	Bremen is Germany's major emigration port. The progres-

sive silting up of the Weser means that the city can no longer use its port for sea-going vessels, and transfers them to other ports on the lower Weser such as Brake and Elsfleth.

1827	Mayor Smidt acquires the site on the city's behalf for its later overseas harbour, Bremerhaven, and construction work starts without delay.
1847	First mail steamer line between Bremerhaven and North America.

1887	Control of the flow of the Weser allows sea-going vessels to return to Bremen's city harbour.
1888	Entry into the German Customs Union and opening of the Free Port.
1920	The city builds an airport.
1944	Air raids destroy 62% of the city and 90% of the port, and 3,852 inhabitants lose their lives.
1945	Bremen and Bremerhaven become the supply ports for the American forces occupying Germany.
1947	Having lost its independence under the Third Reich, Bremen and Bremerhaven become an independent State within federal Germany.
1955	Bremen reaches the figure of half a million - for its population, and for the tonnage of goods handled by its port.
1964	Bremen is connected to the motorway network at the Walsroden interchange.
1967	The container terminal is opened in Neustadt port.
1971	The University of Bremen and the container terminal in Bremerhaven are opened.

Great: Bremen's museums.

Neues Museum Weserburg
Teerhof 20
Germany's biggest museum
of contemporary art.
International art from private collections.
Opening times:
Tuesday to Sunday, 10.00 am to 6.00 pm;
Saturday and Sunday, 11.00 am to 6.00 pm

Kunstsammlungen Böttcherstrasse
Böttcherstrasse 6-10,
Roselius-Haus and
Paula-Becker-Modersohn-Haus.
Opening times: Tuesday to Sunday,
11.00 am to 5.00 pm (no illustration)

Übersee-Museum
Bahnhofplatz 13
The whole world under one roof:
ethnology, natural history,
commerce and trade.
Opening times: Tuesday to
Sunday, 10.00 am to 6.00 pm

Kunsthalle Bremen
Am Wall 207
From Dürer to Picasso
Paintings, graphics, sculpture, from the 14th century to the present day.
Opening times: Wednes-
day to Saturday, 10.00 am
to 5.00 pm; Tuesday,
10.00 am to 9.00 pm

Gerhard-Marcks-Haus
Am Wall 208
North Germany's museum of
sculpture.
Changing exhibitions showing the
sculpture of the 20th century.
Opening times:
Sunday, 10.00 am to 6.00 pm

Focke-Museum
Schwachhauser Heerstrasse 240
The State of Bremen's muse-
um for the history of art and
culture.
Das Museum im Park
History of the State and of
culture, arts and crafts, de-
sign, and archaeology.
Opening times: Tuesday to
Sunday, 10.00 am to 6.00 pm

BREMEN
Be ready for surprises.

Welcome to Bremen!

And a hearty welcome to you as well, the user of this book and visitor to the former Free Hanseatic City. The pictures and text are intended to help you to find your way through the heart of this major city, to find the many sights worth seeing, and to understand their historical context. This is not possible without some knowledge of the city's development, even if its origins are lost in the mists of legend. It is, however, certain that the first settlement, probably inhabited by fishermen and ferrymen, appeared on the Binnenlanddüne, the low hill on the top of which the cathedral now stands. For a long time this was the only dry spot in the midst of a marshy landscape, and it was also attractive because it was the lowest possible crossing-point of the Weser before its estuary opened out; also, the firm ground of the hill reached right down to the river. Thus a settlement of boatsmen and traders grew up here, at the crossing-point of the trade routes along the river and the one crossways to it which ran from the Netherlands to the Elbe. Later, these boatsmen were to venture 70 kilometres downstream and along the North Sea coast, and the settlement inevitably expanded with the aid of piles sunk to support the houses and protective dykes against flooding. These techniques are still relied upon today; Bremen now has 130 kilometres of dykes, and the citizens have to pay their contributions towards maintaining them.

Bremen people, more than the inhabitants of perhaps any other city, lived and still live with their river; even today, it still on the one hand represents the basis of the well-being of the communities, and on the other a constant threat of flooding. This polarity has had its effect on the psychology of the Bremen people; at one and the same time they hang on conservatively to old customs, and also keep their harbour up to the latest state of the technical art. They are both home-minded and open-minded to the whole world, they sound out new possibilities soberly and also open up imaginative new branches of industry. Like most inhabitants of port cities, the Bremener is tolerant and always open-minded towards new ideas, as can be seen from the city's many cultural facilities and from the colourful life in its pubs and cafés for which it is famous.

Anyone who would like to explore the port city should follow the same route as the tour in this book: start with the sights in the city centre. The best starting point is the market square in the centre, which the locals call their „front parlour". The visitor will then, in the last part of his tour, twice cross the former fortification, called the „Wall" in German, which is nowadays a green belt around the city centre, and can then proceed out to the Ostertorviertel, one of the suburbs that sprang up around the city in the 19th century and which it is also well worth exploring on a bicycle. In this way it is possible to discover some of the numerous cycle paths which connect the Hanseatic City with its surrounding area. Other sights are best visited by public transport: the Vegesack district, the artists' village of Worpswede, Teufelsmoor, and Bremerhaven, the Bremen out-port on the Weser estuary. Although 65 kilometres apart and separated from one another by the State of Lower Saxony, these two cities nowadays form the federal State of Bremen, the smallest in our Republic. Although Bremen on its own has more than half a million inhabitants, it has retained a cosy, family atmosphere. Proof of this is provided day in and day out by the numerous guests who flock to its diverse range of hotels of all categories and to many other hotel, catering, and entertainment establishments. Anyone who has ever visited the city will be happy to recommended it to others without restriction.

A walk through Old Bremen

Market square ❶

A walk through Bremen should always start at the point where locals meet; and tourists as well: the market square in the middle of the Old Town. As in the old days, the square is almost entirely enclosed by buildings, but it still reveals glimpses into the neighbouring streets and squares: Domshof, Domsheide, and the churchyard of Our Lady. The visitor can obtain the best view by going over to the Hanseatic cross in the middle of the market square, dominated as it is by one of the most beautiful town halls in the whole of Germany. The western side is partly formed by the historic gable walls of patrician houses such as the Ratsapotheke (1894) and other richly rococo-styled houses at the south-west corner. The other two buildings on that side are modern, but fit in with the Hanseatic style of building and make use of parts of historic buildings. Thus the „Haus am Markt" possesses a doorway dating from about 1600, and the „Deutsches Haus" contains parts of 17th and 18th century façades. The „Schütting" closes the square off to the south-west; it is the centre of Bremen's commercial activities and

Marktplatz is Bremen's market square and "front parlour", with street cafés in front of the historic façades of the town hall and the cathedral.

at the same time a companion building to the town hall opposite, which houses the city's administration and its two mayors. Standing in sharp contrast to these two historic buildings is the modern „Haus der Bürgerschaft", in which Bremen's State and City Parliament meets, and marking the former site of the Bremen stock exchange. The first time any kind of „exchange" was held in this market square was over 300 years ago, under the open sky, so this makes it the oldest stock exchange in Germany. The Marktplatz was sometimes also the focal point of uproar and revolutions, a place of jurisdiction, and also of innumerable festivals and jollities to mark any possible kind of special occasion - such as when the city's First Division football team, Werder Bremen, wins the championship. The team then appears on the town hall balcony before the jubilant crowds.

In front of the town hall's magnificent façade there stands the city's hallmark, the Statue of Roland. There are many

Bremen's hallmark, the Statue of Roland, a symbol of the citizens' love of freedom.

similar statues all over northern Germany, but the distinctive feature of this one is its enormous size (together with its plinth it is more than 10 metres high) and the quality of the artistic work in it. The figure has a youthful, beardless face and a secretive smile, not unlike that on the Mona Lisa. With drawn and upright sword he faces the cathedral and thus symbolises the medieval citizens' striving for liberty against the archbishop's claims to supremacy. Their mistrust was justified, as was confirmed by an action by the archbishop's servants in 1366; they set fire to a wooden predecessor to the present-day statute. The city council therefore had the present statue erected in 1404, later adding the coat-of-arms to emphasise its symbolism. Its inscription can be translated as follows: „Freedom I open unto ye that Karl (the Emperor Charlemagne) and many another prince forsooth granted to this town. And therefore thank ye God, (that) is my counsel." Thus the statue of Roland is still today regarded as a symbol of the Bremener's love of independence, which was safeguarded by their direct loyalty to the Emperor during their Hanseatic past and lasted, with two short interruptions under Napoleon and Hitler, right up to the present day. Thus the belief is still alive in the city-state today that its freedom will be guaranteed just so long as Roland stands on his plinth. He even managed to stay on it during the terrible air raids in 1944/45, because the city council had a wall built round him and filled the space between him and the wall with sand.

The sword was also a symbol in the Middle Ages for jurisdiction by blood, as the severed head at the giant's feet confirms. However, the local inhabitants have their own, highly individual interpretation of this; this is meant to be a memorial to a cripple who laid down his life for the expansion of Bremen. The site of the huge Bürgerpark in those days belonged to Countess Emma, and the city asked her for land because the citizens urgently needed a „common" or open meadowland. She undertook to provide as much land as one man could walk around in one day, but her nephew, who hoped to inherit from her, talked her into choosing a cripple to mark out the land. The cripple summoned up all his strength and managed to mark out 130 hectares - over 300 acres - but the effort was so great that he collapsed and died. As a sign of gratitude, he is now immortalised at the feet of the Statue of Roland.

Peace and plenty flourished in Bremen at the beginning of the 15th century. The city was a member of the Hansa trading league, and had long before been granted its municipal rights, but it was not until about this time that the city council started to plan the construction of their own town hall; in preceding centuries it had only ever met in hired rooms. In order to decide on the size required, the council asked all citizens with voting rights to assemble on the open meadow and form a huge square. The area they took up was marked out with posts and ropes, and its measurements decided the size of the main structure which became this Gothic building (1405- 1407). Four staircase towers, one at each corner, a double row of crenellations, and a defensive walkway over the arched entrance on the market side gave the building the look of a castle close to the centre of the archbishop's power. This symbolism was continued in the form of eight statues on the façade side, which are

The magnificent Renaissance façade of the town hall, facing the market square. In front of it is „Roland the Giant", and in the background the Church of Our Lady.

works breaks it up horizontally. The rich ornamentation and fine statues make their contribution, perfectly harmonising with the Gothic statues under their canopies.

Underneath the breastwork of the balcony there are numerous figures, including, for example, a crowing cock with sceptre and tiara, which refers to the Pope's claims to worldly power. Not far away there is a young woman carrying a nest under one arm containing a hen and chickens. According to legend, some fishermen had been searching during a storm for a place of safety from the rising waters of the Weser, and saw a hen leading her chickens to a higher point on the dunes. They followed her, and founded their settlement there - and this was the origin of Bremen. Nevertheless, some of the chickens did end up in the fishermen's cooking-

Statues of Princes Elector between the windows of the main hall.

still there today; they depict the Emperor, with his imperial insignia, and the seven Princes Elector, as the representatives of worldly sovereignty in the German Empire. The people of Bremen were only prepared to acknowledge this imperial power. In 1600 or thereabouts, after wealthy merchants had had the prestigious „Schütting" building erected, the town council started to consider that the town hall looked somewhat too plain and simple, so the building as it stands today was created in 1616; it is in the Weser Renaissance style, but also including traces of the former Baroque age. The architect, Lüder von Bentheim, was magnificently successful in rejuvenating the existing Gothic structure by means of modern additions, mainly on the market side; the two-storey central addition, crowned by its main gable and supported by the side gables, breaks up the originally monotonous main façade, and the arcaded walk with its two breast-

Town hall façade: the hen and chickens commemorate the legendary founding of the city.

pot. It is perhaps from this traditional tale that a speciality arose which is still to be found on the menus of many a local restaurant, „Bremen farmhouse chicken".

The shorter sides of the old town hall remained very largely unchanged, and embody the Gothic element. On the west side, steps lead down into the Ratskeller or councillors' cellar, created during the conversion work in the early 17th century. Like the Ratskeller in thousands of other towns and cities, this is a favourite meeting-place for Bremen peo-

9

Raktskeller: the view into one of the "Priölken" in the main hall.

ple to take a glass of wine or their mid-day meal, or to recover from strenuous shopping. One particular feature here is the „Priölken", enclosed niches to seat up to five people and particularly suitable for informal meetings. Believe it or not, in this North German port city neither beer nor imported wine is available in the Ratskeller - but, in the neighbouring cellars, there is a stock on hand of more than 600 German wines, including such rarities as a barrel of Rhine wine dating from 1718 and another, the oldest drinkable draught wine, dating from 1653. There are also Mosel wines of the 1723 and 1731 vintages. The passageways through these cellars cover a total of 2 kilometres and stretch out not only to the outer walls of the town hall but also to the foundation walls of the cathedral and the Church of Our Lady. Many rooms, such as the Apostles' Cellar or the Rose Cellar, merely serve for storing wine, others are artistically designed, like the Hauffsaal and the Bacchussaal. This Ratskeller, containing the

world's older collection of wine, combined with the famous Bordeaux wines of the Schütting, is the foundation of Bremen's reputation as possibly the most important wine city in Europe.

Why is there a Ratskeller in Bremen and in so many other medieval cities? The people

Bacchus wine barrel in the vaults of the Ratskeller.

or groups of people who met there over a good glass of wine were perhaps more inclined to agree on a compromise. It was for this reason that, in the Middle Ages, councillors were often elected for their capacity to hold their drink.

At the north-west corner of the town hall,

The town musicians of Bremen, a sculpture by G. Marcks.

the visitor can see the only one of the four original Gothic staircase towers to have been preserved. Below it there is a plinth, almost as tall as a man, and on this plinth is a tower of animals which every German schoolchild immediately connects with Bremen, the „Stadtmusikanten" or town musicians. (They are standing on one another's backs in order to look like a monster and frighten a band of robbers out of their house so as to take it over for themselves, according to a traditional children's story. They are called „Musikanten" because they had left their own homes and become itinerant musicians.)

This picture will confront the observant visitor at many points around the city, but this bronze sculpture, by Professor Gerhard Marcks, is one of the best-quality versions. The new town halls (1909-1915) adjoins to the north; although it is almost twice as big, its skilful architectural design enables it to subordinate itself beneficially to the historic building. Even if only the Upper Hall is open to tourists, out of all the numerous sights worth seeing in the town hall, it is still very much worthwhile going to look at. It takes up the whole of the upper floor of the former town hall, and was mercifully spared damage during the 1944/45 air raids. The tall pointed-arch windows on the short side have been preserved from the Gothic age, and they immerse the hall in bright light. The fittings along the display side dates from the time immediately after the reconstruction, and consist of imaginative early Baroque wood carvings: the artistically fashioned spiral staircase and the luxuriantly designed dividing wall of the two-storey forward building. Hidden behind this is surely the most beautiful room in the whole building, the Güldenkammer; in 1905, the council had its debating chamber redesigned by the Worpswede artist Heinrich Vogeler, a master of the art nouveau period. From the gilded leather wall-hangings, the floor coverings, the cassetted ceiling, to the luxurious furniture, Vogeler here created a perfect composition in the colours of red, gold, and brown. Above the chamber there is a musicians' gal-

Town Hall:
Guided tours: Saturday and Sunday at 11.00 am and 12.00 noon.
May to end of October also: Monday to Friday at 10.00 and 11.00 am and at 12.00 noon.

View through the Upper Hall of the Town Hall. The magnificent interior dates mainly from the time of the reconstruction, in the early 17th century.

lery, where music has been played for centuries to accompany festivities.

The opposite wall contains door-surrounds in various different styles. An outside staircase used to lead from here to the council chamber, but after rebellious citizens had used it in 1531 to burst in on the council it was replaced by the present-day spiral staircase. The twelve „commandments" are inscribed on one door, dating from 1491, which each councillor had to obey, and another door leads

The row of Gothic windows are a reminder of the original Town Hall (about 1400).

to the „Wittheitsstube", or „wisdom room", where mayors met for confidential meetings. This room is connected directly to the Ratskeller, two storeys beneath it, where these great gentlemen could top up any missing wisdom with a drop of fine wine. The doors nowadays lead to the new town hall in which there is also another, larger hall and a beautifully restored reception room.

The only windowless wall is decorated with pictures from various periods; the

13

One of the models of the fine Hansekoggen on the impressive wood-beamed ceiling.

or; also, he sent the first priests here to evangelise Saxony, he defeated the rebellion in Bremen, and he had Willehad anointed as the first Bishop of Bremen. The fact that the city owes its prosperity mainly to sea-faring is documented by the four sailing ships on the impressive wood-beamed ceiling. These „Koggen" were trading ships equipped for warfare, and the models depict the type mainly in service during the Hansa period for warding off pirate attacks.

The two models with the over-sized cannons used to stand in the Schütting, the building which housed the „Kaufmannschaft" or merchants' guild. On festive occasions the cannons were loaded with gunpowder and fired, often resulting in soot all over someone's clothing or a few shattered window-panes. There was thus frequently trouble with citizens complaining that the merchants had been firing off full broadsides late at night with all the windows open. When it was later planned to make the Schütting into a branch of the French administration, the ships were handed over to the town hall to provide company for the two models already there. Together with the candela-

oldest are the frescoes, depicting the wise judge Salomon (1532) and the Emperor Charlemagne and Bishop Willehad in front of the 16th century cathedral. Bremen people feel a particularly close link with Charlemagne because the first documentary record of their city (in 782) refers to the Saxons' rebellion against the Emper-

Town Hall: a glimpse of the luxuriantly decorated Güldenkammer.

bra and the 33 imperial medallions, they now form a magnificent decoration for the ceiling which can be seen at its very best on grand evening occasions. This applies also to the oldest of the festivities that take place here, the „Schaffermahlzeit" (see the chapter on historical events), a dinner which often goes on long into the evening. The spiral staircase on the south side leads down to the Lower Hall, which is just as large, and has dark beams in its ceiling hewn from marshland oak. It is mainly used for exhibitions and theatre performances, and for all its plain and simple appearance is regarded as one of the most beautiful non-church Gothic buildings in northern Germany.

North-westwards from the town hall runs the „Unser Lieben Frauen Kirchhof", once the churchyard of the Church of Our Lady and now used in the mornings as a flower market. It is named after the medieval church which used to have only one main entrance, in the south façade facing the town hall. Its predecessor building had served as long ago as the 11th century as the parish and citizens' church, having been built outside the walls enclosing the area of the bishop's city. The present-day church dates from the 13th century, the choir and the fourth nave on the south side being added in about 1500, as was the unusual main roof, which runs crossways to the naves underneath it, and the decorated gable wall facing the town hall with its buttresses and a dwarf gallery to separate the sandstone masonry of the main wall from the richly stepped brickwork of the gable.

In the north-west corner, the Mesnerhaus is all that is left of the various buildings that used to stand here against the short, broad Roman-style tower (12th century); like the two rounded-arch doorways in the north wall, this formed part of the earlier building. The Gothic north tower was built in the 13th and 14th centuries, but the structure between the towers with the present main entrance did not appear until 1893. The city used to store important documents in the basement, but now this „Tresekammer" serves as a memorial chapel for those who fell in the first world war. As in many Evangelical churches, there is now little remaining of the once sumptuous interior except for remnants of the 15th century wall and ceiling frescoes in the Christopherus room

Equestrian statues of Field Marshal Moltke (before the Church of Our Lady) and of Prince Bismarck (outside the cathedral).

in the upper floor of the southern nave. More recent works worth mentioning are the carved pulpit (18th century), a epitaph to Dietrich von Büren (17th century), and the modern glass in the windows. The interior design has a harmonious effect, in

Fruit and vegetable market on the Domshof, with the Bremer Bank in the background.

keeping with the Westphalian tradition for churches of this kind.

A relief on the outside of the north tower reminds us that many things in Bremen are different from the rest of Germany. This shows the Prussian Field Marshal Moltke on horseback - a form of presentation which in neighbouring Prussia was strictly reserved for reigning princes. It was created in 1909 by the southern German sculptor Hermann Hahn, as was the nearby Marcus fountain.

Passing between the church and the town hall, we come to the largest market square in the city centre, the Domshof (or „cathedral courtyard"). This is the point where, only a few years ago, the modern Neptune fountain set off differences of opinion, and where the last public execution took place, in 1831. The „poison-mixer", a woman called Gesche Gottfried, was put to death under the headsman's axe. No fewer than six bank buildings cluster around this square, the finest of their façades being that of the Bremer Bank, built in the Weser Renaissance style with some art nouveau elements. On closer inspection, this proves to be a branch of the Dresdner Bank, which operates under its own name in virtually all other towns and cities in Germany. As we just said: many things in Bremen are different from the rest of Germany. Thus Prince Bismarck sits in front of the North Tower of the Cathedral, contrary to all the rules of Prussian-dominated Germany, and on horseback at that; moreover, the 6-metre high plinth supporting him places him squarely centre-stage.

The west façade of St Peter's Cathedral, looked at from the market square side again, consists of the 98-metre high twin towers and a connecting building with a Gothic rosette and a triangular gable space. If we allow our glance to wander upwards from the round-arched doorway, we will not find it hard to discern that the work on this building took many centuries, with the architectural taste of the times changing as work progressed. The oldest parts date from the 11th century, when Archbishops Bezelin (1035 to 1043) and Adalbert (1043 to 1072) had a pillar basilica built in the Roman style. Not only the two crypts, under the east and the west Choirs, are preserved from

A view across the market square in front of St Peter's Cathedral, ▶ spiritual centre of the archbishop's power, flanked by the town hall and the once the Haus der Bürgerschaft.

Bronze doorway (19th century) of St Peter's Cathedral.

„Unique to Bremen", page 00), we will enter St Peter's Cathedral through the door in the South Tower. On the right, we pass one of the numerous epitaphs; this one is dedicated to the Dean of the Cathedral Dr Joachim Hincke, who died in 1583. This work, and all the others like it, date from the time after the Reformation, but nevertheless the sheer creative joy of the High Renaissance is expressed here in full. Unlike the north nave opposite, the planned lifting of the vaulted roof was not carried out here; the

St Peter's Cathedral: equestrian statue (ca. 1400).

that time, but also practically all the walls and columns of the lower part of the church. Work began in about 1500 on converting the basilica into a High Gothic church, but retaining most of the substance of the building, but then the Reformation put an end to any building work on the cathedral. It was not until 1888 that a thorough-going renovation project was started which mainly included renovating the two towers; they had been badly damaged by fire and falling masonry. It was at this time that the gable was designed, together with its statues, as well as the statues between the doorways and the bronze doors with their mosaic illustrations of Biblical scenes. They bear huge, magnificently wrought door-knobs in the form of lions' heads (early 13th century).

Whilst the steps and the door of the North Tower enjoy the limelight during the historical custom of „Sweeping the cathedral steps" (see the chapter headed

St Peter's Cathedral:
St Petri Domgemeinde, Sandstrasse 10-12, 28196 Bremen, tel. (0421) 36 50 40. Opening times: Monday to Friday, 10.00 am to 5.00 pm; Saturday, 10.00 am to 12.00 noon; Sunday and public holidays, 2.00 to 5.00 pm.

A view through the central nave of the cathedral in the direction of the east Choir. Opposite the pulpit is a Renaissance tomb.

Reformation intervened. Christ bearing His Cross (1490), the figure behind the High Altar, was the creation of a member of a family of artists who emigrated here from Brabant and were called „Brabander" or „Beldensnyder"; they have left behind a large number of works in this cathedral. The pulpit (1638) is artistically carved, its body from oak and the numerous figures from the more easily worked limewood. The narrow side-chapel immediately behind the pulpit shelters remains of the magnificent choir stalls, dating from 1360 or 1380, which were unthinkingly broken out and torn to pieces in 1822. They depict Biblical scenes and the coats-of-arms of the members of the Cathedral chapter. This governing body was made up of Bremen citizens, and took over responsibility for the administration of the church community in 1636 as well as the possessions and foundations of the cathedral, which up to

then had been in the hands of the bishops and the archbishops; until the period of the Reformation, they had pushed their way steadily into a position of worldly power. Even after the Bremen population had declared itself in favour of the Reformation, in 1522, the Cathedral Chapter initially retained the old confession, and it was not until 10 years later that the populace demanded and was granted its first Evangelical sermon in the time-honoured church building. The archbishop thereupon withdrew from Bremen with his entire retinue, and the cathedral remained locked up until 1547; it was locked up again from 1561 to 1638 as a result of further religious disputes, until the citizenry took the administration of it into its own hands, and responsibility for the repair work as well. The last archbishop in Bremen was the son of King Christian IV of Denmark, and later became King Frederik III, ruling the church-

Artistic cross-ribbed vaulting in the north nave of the Cathedral.

state within the Hanseatic city from 1634 to 1645. He was dismissed by the Swedes, who annexed the cathedral district to the Duchy of Bremen in 1648, when the Thirty Years War came to an end; this in turn belonged to the Kingdom of Sweden. The cathedral district later belonged to Denmark again, and then to England, when the Hannoverians ascended the Britannic throne; finally, in 1803, Napoleon annexed it to the Free Imperial City of Bremen.

Adjoining the last chapel of the southern nave there follows a small room from which a door opens onto the inner courtyard. Here it is worthwhile looking at the figure of a knight (ca. 1400) and the grave of the famous Baron von Knigge, who died in 1796 and had been the representative of the British Crown in Bremen from 1790 onwards. He wrote a famous book, „Über den Umgang mit Menschen" („On Behaviour towards People"), for many years the definitive hand-book on good manners and correct etiquette in genteel circles. A tablet in

the southern crossing is dedicated to the memory of the bishops whose graves were found under the central nave during restoration work between 1974 and 1976. The valuable textiles and grave offerings can now be seen in the neighbouring cathedral museum. Further works of the

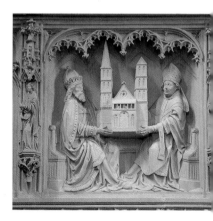

Extract from the bas-relief in the west gallery: Charlemagne with Bishop Willehad and a model of the cathedral.

20

„Beldensnyder" family are preserved on the next pillar and on the pair of pillars beyond it: and epitaph to Dr Brandis and the statues of St Rochus (with plague sores) and the Mother of God.

A luxuriant net-vaulted ceiling arches across the north nave, raised some time after 1500 to the same level as the main nave. Five figures, more than life-sized, in the central „bridal gateway" represent the wise and the foolish virgins; they were originally arranged outside the building. On the two adjoining pillars there are two further epitaphs in the style of the High Renaissance and a somewhat older one at the transition to the North Tower, on which traces of the original paintwork can be seen. Opposite there is an enchanting relief of St Sippe, once again the work of the Beldensnyder family, as is the next bas-relief in front of the organ gallery. The work of this sculptor family reached its rich zenith in this depiction of Charle-

magne and his Bishop Willehad with a model of the cathedral in their hands as it would have appeared in about 1500; this representation is similar to the one in the Upper Hall of the town hall.

A flight of steps leads from in front of the south tower to the west crypt; this is

▲ *Roman-style crucifix on the altar in the east crypt.*

◀ *Silbermann organ in the west crypt.*

21

used nowadays as a chapel for baptisms. In the middle stands a late Roman-style bronze font (ca 1220) which could well be the most valuable item in the whole cathedral. The richly decorated bowl is held aloft by four human figures, each astride a prostrate lion. The works of art here stretch back into the 11th century; the depiction of Christ in Majesty (1047), a Roman-style grave panel with three bishops' staffs, and the artistic capitel with typically Italian ornamentation and

Magnificent pillars and bundles of columns in the central nave of the cathedral.

Modern choir screen with figures from the salvation story (upper row) and from worldly history.

figures. This is the work of the Lombardine sculptors whom Archbishop Adalbert brought back to Bremen with him in 1047 on his return from Italy. The only item of more recent date is the small organ, but it was made by one of the most famous organ-builders in Germany, Gottfried Silbermann.

From the northern crossing we descend into the east crypt, which together with the west crypt is the oldest structure in Bremen, remaining almost unchanged throughout the centuries; it can thus breath the full breath of the Roman period in its earliest years. Whilst checkerboard ornamentation reveals Italian influence, German symbols from pre-Christian times such as the Fenris wolf and the Midgard snake stand in apparent contradiction of the early Christian symbol of the open blossom. Of the four memorials grouped around the grave of Archbishop Adalbert, who died in 1072, three are once again products of the Beldensnyders' workshop (ca 1500): Christ as the Bearer of our pain, and the two crucifixes.

Both floors of the neighbouring southeast chapel have been arranged as the cathedral museum, which is definitely worth a visit for the grave finds of 1974-76 alone. Painstaking restoration work was devoted to the textiles, centuries old, but they are very sensitive to light and have to be kept in a heavily darkened room. The grave finds are to be seen behind glass: parts of the ornaments with which the bishops were buried as well as rings, parts of the bishops' staffs, chalices, and communion dishes. The other rooms of the museum hold archi-

Cathedral museum:
bishops' staff (ca. 1300).

Cathedral museum:
bas-relief "Abendmahl" (ca. 1500).

tectural fragments from the Roman age, bas-reliefs, statues, and liturgical vessels dating from 1400 onwards, documentation on all the bishops and archbishops of Bremen, and finds from the most recent archaeological excavations. The visitor can also see Bremen's oldest relic with writing on it: a lead tomb plaque for Bishop Lenderich, who died in 845. A bas-relief is dedicated to the doctor-saints, Cosmas and Damian, and their good works. The reliques of the martyrs, greatly respected in the Middle Ages, had been brought from Rome by Archbishop Adaldag in 965, thus greatly raising the respect in which the cathedral was held. From 1400 onwards, the reliques were kept in a valuable silver shrine, but the

cathedral Chapter sold this, complete with its contents, to Bavaria in 1648.

In the „Lead Cellar", which lies slightly off to one side of the main building, and can be reached via the inner courtyard, there is another Bremen curiosity awaiting the visitor; he can quietly contemplate eight mummified bodies in their glass-topped coffins. The oldest is that of a roofing tiler who fell to his death from one of the towers in 1450. As he came from outside Bremen, his coffin was placed in the Lead Cellar where his working material had been stored, lead sheeting from the roof. It was not until a few years later that his coffin was rediscovered, having been forgotten about; it was opened, and the body was found to be merely mummified. It was later joined by

Information

Cathedral museum: Opening times: Monday to Friday, 10.00 am to 5.00 pm (but from November to April only from 1.00 to 4.30 pm); Saturday, 10.00 am to 12.00 noon; Sunday and public holidays, 2.00 to 5.00 pm.
Lead Cellar: Opening times from 2nd May to 31st October as for St Peter's Cathedral.
Tower ascents: 2nd May to 31st October, Monday to Friday, 10.00 am to 5.00 pm. Saturday 10.00 am to 12.00 noon; Sunday and public holidays 2.00 to 5 pm.

A view into the Lead Cellar with two of the coffins.

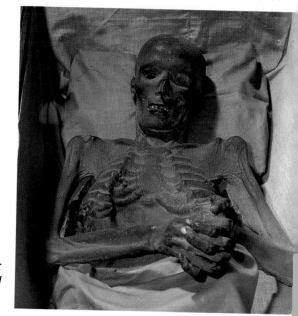

Lead Cellar: coffin with mummified body.

the body of the English Lady Stanhope, who died in 1590, and then in the middle of the 17th century by a Swedish general together with his adjutant and a Swedish countess; in the following century there also came a student, an English Major, and the only native of Bremen, a workman called Konrad Ehlers. As with the roofer, and with later attempts involving dead animals, the Lead Cellar proved to have the property of conserving dead bodies by desiccation. This can only be explained by the extraordinarily dry air in the room built on top of the dune. Generations of sacristans have earned themselves a small tip now and then by showing visitors the way to the mummies.

265 steps lead upwards to a point about half way up the 98-metre high towers, but the visitor is more than rewarded by the magnificent view.

The modern Haus der Bürgerschaft closes off the market square to the east. Right at the top is the plenary chamber for the 100 parliamentarians. The Bremen Bürgerschaft, which is equivalent to a State parliament, consists of 20 delegates from Bremerhaven and 80 from Bremen itself, the latter being at the same time the city council. All the delegates vote to select the Senate, which is in effect the ministers, and they in turn elect two out of their own number to be the two mayors, one of whom is then also the President of the Senate.

The Schütting is the traditional home of all commercial activity in Bremen and stands almost symbolically in the city centre in between the town hall and the River Weser. On the bank alongside it, near the Schnoorviertel, there used to be

The Schütting is the prestigious home of the Chamber of Commerce and Industry and stands in Bremen's market square.

a harbour on the Balge, a navigable side-arm of the Weser which was later filled in. Initially it was used for landing fish and other seafood for sale in the nearby markets and later in those further inland. It is no accident that Europe's biggest trade fair for the fish industry takes place in Bremen. As long ago as the 13th century, beer was being exported from here, and the ships brought luxurious cloth back on the return journey; from the 17th century onwards they also brought Bordeaux wines. Trade flourished particularly once America had been discovered. In addition to the importation and resale of coffee, tobacco, cocoa, citrus fruits, and exotic spices, it was soon discovered that these goods could be processed, and coffee-roasting mills and ci-

Schütting can be regarded as a counter-weight, standing opposite the town hall. At the time when it was built, in the late Gothic style (1537-38), the council was still meeting in its very plain early Gothic building. When the merchants added the central gable and the balustrade as decoration to their building, some time before 1600, as well as the graceful coronation over the windows, the gentlemen in the town hall decided on a very thorough modernisation of their building. However, the merchants improved the appearance of the main façade of their building as well during the course of the centuries, so that it can still compete with the town hall even today. Thus the Renaissance doorway was built in 1896-98 with an inscription which has always been

Valuable Chamber of Commerce table silver in the Schütting.

gar, cigarette, and chocolate factories soon sprang up, most of them still in existence today. They gave rise to a prosperous and self-confident merchant class which struggled not only for the independence of the city but also deliberately entered into competition with the city council. It is for this reason that the

the motto of the merchants: „Buten und binnen, wagen und winnen", which in Low German means: „Inside and outside, venture and win". The central gable is decorated by a medieval „Kogge" under full sail. The gable side, on the other hand, still presents the original 16th century structure almost unaltered. The east ga-

A busy summer's day in the market between the statue of Roland and the harmonious row of old patrician houses.

The magnificent Renaissance gable of the former city weighbridge in Langenstrasse.

ble displays the classical forms of the early Renaissance, whilst the western stepped gable with its stone lions still embodies Gothic architecture.

The Schütting marks the end of Langenstrasse, once the main road through the merchants' quarter, where it enters the market square. The corner house on the right is a newly built bank, but it has had a fine Baroque façade placed in front of it. The next buildings along the street also belong to the bank, which built the historic door surrounds and a bronze tablet showing this row of houses in the 17th century into them. The same applies to the neighbouring building, the former city weighbridge, with its impressive Renaissance gable. Lüder von Bentheim, who was later

to be the architect who renovated the town hall, was commission by the town to erect this building for them with its four main floors and three attic floors. In addition to the usual forms used in gable design, the architect also worked with alternating bricks and grey sandstone. A coat-of-arms with the key of the city and a pair of golden scales have restored the building, after the destruction of wartime, to the glory it possessed before uniform weights were introduced and private weighbridges were officially approved and calibrated. Prior to that time, the only official way of determining weights, for merchants, customers, and taxpayers, was with the public scales or weighbridge, operated by court-sworn weighmasters and their clerks and servants.

Böttcherstrasse ➋

Passing by the Schütting along the street of the same name, we can branch off to the right and finally leave the market square. At the end of the building we are greeted by a golden boy above the entrance to Böttcherstrasse; he is the „Bringer of Light", and represents the first of a number of surprises which this street has to offer. It was once the direct link from the market to the River Weser, and thus a good selling position for craftsmen, particularly the coopers - „Böttcher". Their barrels stood by the hundred on the decks of sailing ships, filled with such things as fresh water, beer, wine, or rum, or else salted meat, fish, and other foodstuffs, and even „ship's biscuit", the daily bread of ships' crews.

lazy men"), but on the left is the unconventional Paula-Becker-Modersohn-Haus (1926/27) showing the architectonic escapades of which the Worpsweder sculptor Bernhard Hoetger was capable. In the centre of the entrance hall is a statue, „Mother with Child", likewise a work by Hoetger, as is the „Bringer of Light" at the entrance to the street. Shops are grouped around this entrance hall offering arts and crafts for sale, and from here the visitor can reach the inner Craftsmen's Courtyard. As its name suggests, craftsmen such as goldsmiths, glass-blowers, and potters work in the workshops alongside. In the middle of this small courtyard Hoetger placed his „Fountain of the seven lazy men", with the figures of the Bremen Town Musicians on the foun-

The „Bringer of Light" at the entrance to Böttcherstrasse.

When the harbour had to be transferred northwards in the 16th century, because the Weser was silting up, this street lost its attractiveness. From 1902 onwards, a Mr Roselius, coffee merchant and benefactor of the arts (and inventor of decaffeinated coffee), bought up all the houses one by one in this 100-metre long street and converted them, with the aid of three architects, into a cultural centre. The right-hand row starts with familiar historical shapes at the Sieben-Faulen-Haus (the „house of the seven

tain outlet. Whilst they have achieved international fame, the characters who gave their name to this fountain, depicted by the artist as self-satisfied, over-fed gentlemen, are only known in the surrounding area of Bremen. This is probably the origin of the legend of the seven farmer's sons who were too lazy to fetch water from the Weser and therefore sank a well; they then laid out the road with cobblestones, because they were too lazy to pull their cart out of the mud when it became stuck; and

A view through the architectonically delightful Böttcherstrasse, famous for its extensive art collections.

planted trees around their house because they were too lazy to walk to the forest. Hoetger, like many Bremen people, realised that this brand of laziness was perfectly well worth copying, and spurred many people on to make rational progress. This was probably also the view of his client, Mr Roselius, to whom Hoetger erected a discreet memorial in this courtyard.

In the Paula-Becker-Modersohn-Haus, the merchant mainly honours the Worpsweder artist of (almost) the same name who died at the early age of 31 and whose work had not yet met with any real appreciation in the 1920's. However, Roselius collected her pictures, drawings, and sketches and gave them an impressive setting with this house. The upper rooms of the building he created are dedicated to the works of Bernhard Hoetger, who without any doubt set the clearest accents in the Böttcherstrasse.

In the Roselius-Haus next door, this benefactor has accommodated his collection of brilliant artistic pieces, as well as books and sculptures by Low German artists of the 14th to the 18th centuries. A further point of attraction is the silver treasure of the „Company of the Black Heads from Riga", a Bremen foundation of the Hansa period. It is also well worth seeing the gigantic patrician house itself (1588), as its large number of prestigious rooms never fail to excite the visitor. The St Peters house opposite, dedicated to the patron saint of Bremen, houses a number of restaurants and the gambling casino.

On the left, the Böttcherstrasse opens out into St.-Petrus-Platz, which is thronged with visitors every day at 12.00 noon and 3.00 and 6.00 pm because that is when the carillon starts to play on the Roman-style gable. The bells, of Meissen porcelain, play a sequence of

Art collections in Bremen's Böttcherstrasse:
Paula-Becker-Modersohn-Haus / Roselius-Haus, tel. (0421) 33 65 077.
Opening times: Tuesday to Sunday, 11.00 am to 5.00 pm.
Coopers' Carillon every day at 12.00 noon, 3.00 and 6.00 pm.

▲ B. Hoetger: Roselius   ▼ St. George (silver)   ▲ Prestigious reception room   ▼ Cupola in

saal *Paula Becker-Modersohn: "Armenhäuslerin"* ▼   *St. Mauritius (gilded silver)* ▲

sea-shanties while the central part of the tower rotates and the portraits of famous conquerors of the oceans appear on 10 colour wooden panels, from the Viking Leif the Fortunate and Columbus to Lindbergh and Count Zeppelin. Starting from an idea of Roselius', Hoetger once again produced the carvings, as in the neighbouring Haus Atlantis. Named after the part of the world which, as fable has it, sank beneath the waves, it contains in its interior an open spiral staircase which leads up to the „Himmelssaal" or „Sky hall". Roselius originally housed his extensive prehistoric collection here, but this has since been enlarged and transferred to Worpswede.

Together with this building, which now belongs to a chain of hotels, the Robinson Crusoe House forms the final narrow alley of the Böttcherstrasse. In sharp contrast to the modern building, the half-timbered building with its upper floors jutting far out forwards takes the visitor far back into the past, to the days of Robinson Crusoe's adventure. In the original version of the novel, Robinson's family was to have been called Kreutzner and to have left Bremen for Hull, in England. The gilded heads on the façade arouse curiosity as to the interior of the building, in the staircase of which carved and brightly painted wooden panels relate Robinson's adventures. The Böttcherstrasse in Bremen is famous as a street of artists and craftsmen, but it also house a number of other elegant shops and hospitable taverns which form part of the night-life of the old town centre.

▲ *Böttcherstrasse:*
carillon made of Meissen porcelain.

Carved wooden panels show ▶
famous conquerors of the oceans.

34

On the Martinianleger

At the end of the Böttcherstrasse we come out onto the busy Martinistrasse, named after St Martin's church towering up on the right. A tunnel leads us to the Martinianleger, a jetty from which boat trips on the lower Weser start as well as tours round the harbour lasting 75 minutes.

The left bank of the Weser is formed here by an island called Teerhofinsel, separated from the mainland by the Kleine Weser. Just short of the point where they meet at the Bürgermeister Smidt bridge, the former premises of a coffee-roasting company have been converted to house the New Weserburg Museum, dedicated to collecting international contemporary art from about 1960 onwards; this gives it the right to claim to be „protecting the aura of the original". Rotating exhibition of the highest quality have earned this museum, which is still relatively young, a considerable reputation in expert circles.

New Weserburg Museum: man at window.

Beyond the island is the Alte Neustadt, an extensive industrial area in which a number of well known firms are to be found (they produce coffee, chocolate, and beer). The two major breweries are heirs to a 700-year-old Bremen tradition of exporting beer, and account between them for about 50% of Germany's total export quantity of bottled beer.

Not far beyond the Stephani and the railway bridges, on the right, is the Weser railway station with its 500-metre long „Kaje". Because the average reach of the tide (from the high water to the low water mark) is a good 3.30 metres, this embankment had to be built very high, and it was an expensive undertaking. Behind it are some of the sidings totalling 315 kilometres in length which are laid in the city harbour of Bremen alone. As the water depth in this section is only 6 metres, the mooring here is no more suitable for large ships than is the Hohentorhafen, which slices into the land on the left bank of the Weser. Behind it is the site covered by a grain-processing company and a major engineering factory, and on the left is the start of the Weseruferpark. On the next tongue of land, on the right, the average water depth is 10 metres, which means that sea-going vessels can float in to the Europahafen. This boasts a modern RoRo (roll-on/roll-off) loading facility and container loading jetties, the hallmark of today's Bremen

---

 Information

75-minute boat trip round the harbour: *Depart from Martinianleger (access by pedestrian tunnel at the end of Böttcherstrasse) from March to end of October, every day at 11.30 am, 1.30 and 3.15 pm; April to end September also at 10.00 am and 2.45 pm. November to February on request, Tel. 0421/ 321229.*

New Weserburg Museum: *Bremen P9 Teerhof 20, tel. (0421) 59 83 90, fax (0421) 50 52 47. Opening times: Tuesday to Friday, 10.00 am to 6.00 pm; Saturday and Sunday, 11.00 am to 6.00 pm; closed on Mondays*

View from Teerhofinsel across the Weser to the city centre, with the late Gothic St Martin's church, built in the 13th century as a church for merchants

and seamen. It was given its present form with the four transverse roofs between 1376 and 1384.

Vulkan yard: various phases in the construction of ships in the floating and dry docks.

which, combined with computer control, ensures a rapid transhipment of goods and thus a quick turn-round time for the ships. Europahafen, built between 1885 and 1888, as well as the Überseehafen beyond it, lies „outside Germany" for customs purposes, i.e. the goods do not go through customs until they leave the fenced-in port area by land or water. The quays in the Überseehafen total 3 kilometres in length, and this is where most of the cranes for handling mixed cargoes are to be found, as well as the gigantic warehouses, one of which is a large refrigerated and deep-freeze store. Lying parallel behind it (and now „inside Germany") is the Holz- und Fabrikhafen („wood and factory harbour") and the Getreidehafen („grain harbour") with its enormous silos which can hold a total of 250,000 tonnes. They are filled and emptied, with a minimum of dust being created, by three elevators which together can move 1,000 tonnes per hour.

Sailing out into the Weser we can see the floating docks and shipyards on the right which used to belong to a firm simply called Weser AG. It was once Bremen's biggest yard, and built numer-

ous major ships; one of these was the Bremen IV, in 1928, a luxurious passenger ship, and another was a giant tanker of 300,000 gross registered tonnes. Bremen nowadays has only one major yard, Vulkan, which works on a strip of the bank north of Vegesack. Behind the Werfthafen is the wide area of the Industriehafen, which is insulated from the tides by a lock 170 metres long. Some of the seven harbour basins specialise in particular types of cargo, such as the Hüttenhafen, where raw material is landed for the Klöckner iron foundries and its finished products are shipped out, and the other harbours for petroleum, coal, and potash. On the left bank of the Weser is the Neustädter Hafen, the most modern of all the port facilities within Bremen proper. In addition to a RoRo and other modern loading facilities for containers and mixed cargoes, it boasts the largest storage capacity both in enclosed warehouses and on its enormous open-air storage areas. This harbour is once again outside the customs area; and, at 11 metres, its basin is the deepest.

No visitor to Bremen should search around these port facilities for the „romantic" side of seafaring. Instead, he will find ultra-modern computer-controlled technology, a hi-tech operation which is continuing to work towards giving its customers the best possible attention with high-precision organisation and perfect service. Bremen has succeeded here, despite somewhat difficult times, in keeping hold of about 100,000 jobs directly or indirectly dependent on its port. This includes, for instance, the Bremen Cotton Exchange, which has been in existence since 1872 and is part of the „Fibres Institute of Bremen, and the German-Indonesian Tobacco Exchange; both of these institutions influence the quality of these imported goods by providing expert assessments and helping to set the price.

The Schnoor ❹

From the Martinianleger we can follow the signs in the direction of „Schnoor". Once we have passed the Wilhelm Kaisen bridge, they lead us under the „Tiefer", a main traffic road, directly into this medieval-looking district of the city. Its name comes from the German word for „string", and its narrow houses really do look as if they were strung along together.

Original stone plaque with Will in the Kolpingstrasse.

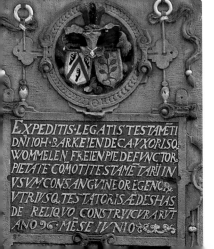

A former hearthstone used to drain off rainwater and as an escape-route for cats.

This is the place where originally fishermen and sailors settled, building their wooden houses on little hills called „Warften" because of the constant danger of flooding. As long ago as the 8th century they maintained a ferry link across the Weser, and the first bridge followed in the 13th century. Craftsmen and traders later settled on the island; it is formed by the Weser and its side-arms, the Balge and the Klosterbalge. The owners of the houses directly alongside the navigable Balge were allowed, for a fee, to build their latrines out over the water in a construction similar to an oriole, thus inventing the flushing toilet. Nevertheless, there were sometimes complaints from sailors who requested that these toilets should not be used just when a ship was passing by. As the other inhabitants of the island also threw their soil, and that of their domestic animals, into this arm of the river, and the sailors anchoring here in Bremen's oldest harbour of course did the same, the city discovered that it was necessary to clean the Balge out thoroughly and regularly - once every 60 years or so.

In the 16th and 17th centuries, however, the Schnoor had become a desirable residential district even for citizens of considerable standing, as can be seen from a number of richly decorated hous-

In the Schnoor:
the alley with the same name
as Bremen's most romantic dis-
trict.

es with their typical oriole windows. In the 19th century, many of them moved out into the (then) modern, leafy suburbs, and craftsmen, labourers, and shopkeepers moved into the Schnoor. The district underwent its last major change from 1959 onwards, when the Bremen city parliament decided to renovate it thoroughly but without losing the historical architecture. With the aid of the house owners its succeeded in modernising this district in such a way that the interiors of the houses were attractive to live in but the medieval charm of the district was not endangered. Nowadays, the Schnoor and its 100 houses on only 2.2 hectares (5½ acres) is one of the most popular tourist attractions in the city, but it has nevertheless not degenerated into a museum; alongside the old houses there are innumerable artists' studios, art galleries, antique dealers, grocery shops,

cafés, restaurants, and cosy taverns creating a unique atmosphere.

Anyone who strolls through the narrow alleys will discover original details with every step: keystones with the date of construction and fanciful decorations, pretty statues and carvings, memorial plaques, porches, door surrounds. A fountain in Stavendamm commemorates a former bath-house, and a bronze memorial an original Bremen character, Heini Holtenbeen (1835 to 1909). He was given this nickname („wooden leg", in Low German) because he fell through a skylight when he was an apprentice and suffered not only head injuries but also the loss of one leg. His humorous remarks gave rise to many anecdotes, and the association for the conservation of the Schnoor calls itself the „Schnoor-Verein Heini Holtenbeen" and honours him with this memorial and with a tombstone in the Oberneuland cemetery. Another fountain, the „Ottjen-Alldag-Brunnen", refers to a character in a novel by the local Bremen author Georg Droste, who lost his eyesight at the age of 20 and spent his life as a basket-maker. He related stories he had made up for himself while he worked, and his children wrote them down. The memorial shows Ottjen Alldag in the net of the cords of fate, linked with an epitaph to the blind writer. A statue in front of the Packhaus in a street called „Wüste Stätte" is dedicated to St James the Elder. This apostle was executed by King Herod because of his missionary activities, and legend relates that his followers placed his body in a boat which drifted all the way to the coast of Spain, where he had spent time teaching and preaching. There he was buried, and in the 11th or 12th century a magnificent cathedral was built over his grave; from then on Compostela was called Santiago (St James) de Compostela. Apart from Rome and Jerusalem, his grave was the place most visited by Christian pilgrims, who travelled there by land and by water. Innumerable ships also brought pilgrims there from Bremen, which helped the seamen and the taverners to earn money. It is therefore no wonder that the Hanseatic city gratefully erected a memorial to the patron saint of pilgrims. The Packhaus is so called because it used to serve as a store; today it is the home of the „Theater im Schnoor", which presents plays, cabarets, and small works, and a doll and marionette theatre.

On the edge of the Schnoor, alongside Balgebrückstrasse, is the only former abbey church to have been preserved in Bremen. It was built in the 14th century in the North German brick Gothic style for the beggar Order of the Franciscans. After the Reformation, the church came into the possession of the City of Bremen, which made it available as a reserve church for minorities, and in 1816 handed it over to its Catholic community. The Catholics had it thoroughly renovated in 1823 which included adding a vault and raising the floor by 3 metres on account of the constant danger of flooding. The west front is particularly well worth seeing; it is regarded as a masterpiece of brick architecture.

Continuing up-hill we reach the Dechanatstrasse from there the Ostertorstrasse,

Row of houses in the Schnoor, with St John's church in the background.

Statue of St James the Elder in front of the Packhaus.

along which we move away from the nearby cathedral. The left-hand side of the street is dominated by the massive buildings of the law-courts and the central police station, typically monumental structures of the time of the last Kaiser Wilhelm. The next main road marks the course of the former town walls, long since demolished, to which the bailey, moat, embankment, and gun-emplacements were connected. The parks and gardens which have replaced them are interrupted by the looming **Kunsthalle** ❺, built between 1847 and 1849 and rebuilt in 1900. This art gallery contains some significant European paintings of the 15th century and onwards, and sculptures dating from the 17th and later centuries, a library of the history of art, and one of Europe's largest collections of etchings. The first of the 40 or so exhibition rooms is devoted to the Worpswede masters, and the hall on the upper floor to the painter Paula Becker-Modersohn. The significance of the collection becomes all the clearer when one knows that it was created by a private art society, the Bremer Kunstverein of 1823; it is, incidentally, one of the oldest in Germany, and here in Bremen it has worked wonders.

A little further on, the two identical **Ostertorwachhäuser** ❻ or watchmen's houses mark the position of the old eastern gate. It was replaced in 1825 by a prison and customs house. The right-hand guardhouse is now the Gerhard-Marcks-Haus and houses works by the Bremen sculptor who created the „town musicians" in front of the town hall. In addition to this, the museum organising rotating exhibitions of modern sculpture and graphics and has a studio workshop in which courses are offered in drawing, printing graphics, modelling, and sculpture.

Kunsthalle: the Bremer Kunstverein has assembled many significant works here.

One of the Ostertor guardhouses (1825), now the Gerhard-Marcks-Haus.

Kunsthalle: Am Wall 207. tel. (0421) 32 90 80, fax (0421) 32 90 847. Opening times: Tuesday to Sunday, 10.00 am to 5.00 pm (but until 9.00 pm on Tuesday); closed on Monday. **User times for the etchings room:** Tuesday, 10.00 am to 6.00 pm. **Gerhard-Marcks-Haus:** Am Wall 208 (Alte Ostertorwache), tel. (0421) 32 72 00, fax (0421) 33 78 675. Opening times: Tuesday to Sunday, 10.00 am to 6.00 pm; closed on Monday

Information

In the Ostertorviertel

Once we have passed the guardhouses we are in the Ostertorviertel, Bremen's best-known suburb. Three of the five municipal theatres are clustered together on **Goetheplatz** ❼: the Theater am Goetheplatz (for opera, operetta, and musicals), the Schauspielhaus (for plays and ballets), and the cosy little Brauhauskeller (for small-cast plays and readings - the name actually means „brewery cellar"). Set back on the right from the Theater am Goetheplatz there stands the late-Classic style Villa Ichon (1849), the striking features of which are the rich decoration of its façades and ceilings. It is used nowadays for various grand cultural and social events.

This is the start of the Ostertorsteinweg, a street of boutiques and shops with something for every taste and thus „Bremen's secret High Street". A short diversion

Classic-style façade of the Theater am Goetheplatz; in front of it is the Maskenmann sculpture.

Typical Bremen houses:
Beim Paulskloster,
a street in the Milchquartier.

through the **Milchquartier** ❽ leads us through Mittelstrasse, where we turn left into Beim Paulskloster and Köpkenstrasse before returning to the main shopping street. This diversion provides an object-lesson in how to create a harmonious overall appearance in rows of houses, even though they are fitted in very closely together, by designing each façade individually. Most of the inhabitants of the Milchquartier are ordinary working people, so the houses they live in are not particularly elaborate. However, as a residential district its appealing feature is the living greenery in the front gardens and its idyllic remoteness from the hurly-burly of the city.

Returning to Ostertorsteinweg - as its name suggests, it was one of the first roads to be given a cobblestone surface - we will travel a little further away from the city centre before turning off left into Blumenstrasse. A fine group of suburban Bremen houses is waiting for us in the next street, Kreftingstrasse, which were built between 1860 and 1863 to house leading Bremen families and are now scheduled monuments because they typify the best kind of Bremen housing. The typical features are the two-storey and three-storey façades of these terraced houses, which have an apparently low-sunk basement floor on their street sides; only apparently, because they were only created when the streets were built up to a higher level. On their garden sides, the whole face of this lower floor is visible and each has a door at ground level. Ac-

cordingly, this lower floor can be used as partly cellars or a laundry, partly as kitchens and toilets. The next higher floor accommodates the living, dining, and reception rooms, and above that are the bedrooms, with sleeping accommodation for the domestic staff at the very top. Because they were designed as large single-family houses, and there is little possibility of dividing them up into separate flats, these Bremen houses have proved very attractive to communities of students and other young people, and an unusually high proportion of them live in this district.

Leaving Kreftingstrasse, we follow the broad, busy Am Dobben to the next cross-roads where we turn off to the right into Humboldtstrasse and then immediately left into **Mathildenstrasse** ❾. Building work started here in 1869 under the architect Rutenberg, and he named the street after his wife. It is now regarded as one of the finest suburban streets to have been preserved, boasting some particularly successful examples of architectonic design such as Nos. 94, 99, and 100. The citizens who lived here were prosperous, and for them an artistically designed façade front to the street was just as important as a sumptuous interior.

We can now go along Feldstrasse and come out on Am Dobben, where we turn left and then immediately right into Bohnenstrasse in order to reach Gertrudenstrasse. From here, a passage leads into a particularly well designed courtyard, **Auf den Höfen** ❿, where not only the small shops and craftsmen's studios but also

Street café on Ostertorsteinweg

Row of houses in "Am Dobben".
Figures decorate a patrician house.

Bremen houses with storm porch.
Wealthy citizen's house: Mathildenstr. 14.

the cosy taverns attract customers. It is younger people in particular who feel themselves drawn here as if by magic, although there are plenty of other places in the Ostertorviertel where night-life flourishes in cafés, bars, and taverns, particularly as there is no „closing time" at week-ends.

Another passage leads us back out onto Auf den Häfen, where we turn right. At the end of this street we keep half-left and follow Imre-Nagy-Weg in the direction of the city centre. Where this opens out into Präsident-Kennedy-Platz there is the practical modern building of the **Staatsarchiv ⓫**. Its main entrance is graced by a nicely executed coat-of-arms dated 1591 with the Bremen key, a symbol both of the patron saint and of the inhabitants; they regard it as the key to the world and relate it to the harbour which is their lifeblood and an important instrument for safeguarding their homely remoteness.

After crossing the city moat we enter the Wallanlage, and go along one of the paths past a bronze group entitled „Rosselenker" (1902). Crossing the next road, Herdentor, our glance will fall on a fine

The mill in the Wallanlage is the hallmark of these parks and gardens encircling the city centre.

„Der Rosselenker" a sculpture by Tuaillon (1902) in the Wallanlage.

Swineherd with dog and sows („Sögen" in Low German), and group of figures at the entrance to Sögestrasse.

windmill, one of the hallmarks of Bremen, before heading back into the city centre. The way there is along **Sögestrasse** ⓬ - the name means „Sows' street", and we are reminded of this by a bronze group depicting pigs and their swineherd and his dog. This name, as well as that of Herdentor („Herdsmen's gate"), comes from the numerous domesticated animals which passed this way in the old days travelling to and from the nearby Bürgerweide („Citizens' meadow").

The street here nowadays lies in the middle of the main shopping centre, which spreads out to the right and the left of it. In the Lloyd-Passage and the recently opened Katharinenkloster-Passage, both of which are roofed over, a session of window-shopping is a real pleasure even when the whether is inclement. We can thus finish our tour not by heading straight back to the market square but with a diversion through the Lloyd-Passage (second turning on the right) to its end in Papenstrasse and then into Obernstrasse (left again).

Roofed-in shopping street in the city centre: the Lloyd-Passage.

Outside the city centre

Whilst the main sights to see are in the old city centre and the Ostertorviertel, and are covered by our tour, we would now like to mention some of the other sights worth seeing in this Hanseatic city.

special events. This is swamped with people day and night during the international 6-day cycle races, which take place in January every year and are a great event not only from the sports point of view. In 1993 the building was extended to include the CCB, the modern Congress Center Bremen, thus making it a partic-

Überseemuseum: central hall with models of boots and huts from the South Seas.

The **Überseemuseum** in the square in front of the mainline railway station exhibits not only a fine ethnological collection but also numerous exhibits of natural and trading history from all parts of the world. Plenty of space is also accorded to the evolution of living creatures up to the era of modern Man.

Just behind the northern exit from the station is where the **Bürgerweide** starts, surrounded by extensive municipal buildings such as the ice stadium and the **Stadthalle**, a centre for cultural and other

ular point of attraction for trade fairs and congresses as well.

The **Bürgerpark** adjoins to the north-east. It was designed 130 years ago by Bremen citizens and since then has been maintained and cared for by private donations. Quiet paths lead past canals and lakes and across broad meadows and woodland groves. Seekers after recreation and leisure sporting activities will find an ideal site for their purposes here; coffee-shops, a restaurant, a beer-garden, and the exclusive Park Hotel invite the visitor to rest and relax.

Übersee-Museum:
Bahnhofsplatz 13, tel. (0421) 361-9176.
Opening times: Tuesday to Sunday, 10.00 am to 6.00 pm; closed on Monday.

▲ Bürgerpark:
   Hollersee with Park Hotel

Autumn breaths golden ▶
colours across the Stadtwald.

▼ Viehweide: a meadow for cat-
   tle in the Bürgerpark, with the
   Meierei (creamery) beyond it.

On the other side of the railway line, the **Bürgerpark** becomes the Stadtwald, a stretch of woodland through which long-distance runners can enjoy the naturally springy forest floor beneath their feet as they follow the „Finnbahn" route. Beyond that, the lake variously known as Unisee (because it is alongside the University) or Stadtwaldsee attracts not only swimmers and wind-surfers but also campers and caravanners.

North-west of the centre, at Waller Heerstrasse 165, is one of the largest theatres in the city, the **Ernst-Waldau-Theater,** which presents mainly folk-plays in the North German dialect, Low German (Plattdeutsch), but also comedies and other plays from all parts of world literature, some of them translated into Low German. The side-rooms of the theatre are sued for events of all kinds: exhibitions, readings, the friendly morning discussions known as Frühschoppen (an „early glass of wine"), theatre balls, and children's theatre.

Upstream on the Weser, the **Osterdeich** attracts thousands of Bremen people for a walk on fine weekends. In the big cross-ways street on the left, Sielwall, we will find the **MOKS-Theater,** which is part of the Bremer Theater and entirely organised with schoolchildren and young people in mind. Continuing along Osterdeich we come to the **Weserstadion** on the right, the home ground of the First Division football team Werder Bremen SV; it forms part of the Peterswerder complex, a gigantic area with sports facilities of every imaginable kind.

The „Werder" is the (almost-)island opposite, where there is also the **Planetarium** with public lectures in the evenings (on Wednesdays at 7.30 pm in the six winter months, with views of the stars when the weather permits). On the other side of the island and the side-arm, the Kleine Weser, is the Leibnitzplatz and another theatre, the **Bremen Shakespeare Company,** which has dedicated itself totally to the Bard's works. The simplest way to reach the **Focke-Museum**, the Bremen State Museum for the History of Art and Culture in the Schwachhauser Heerstrasse, is by bus. Its four buildings show exhibits from Bremen's past, including prehistoric and early historic finds and of course the histo-

Bremer Landesmuseum (Focke-Museum): model of a „Kogge".

ry of seafarers. The faience-tiled ovens and the collections of porcelain and silver offer an impressive view of life in the better class of Hanseatic merchant families.

Not far away, in an extension of the Heerstrasse, the **Rhododendronpark** attracts thousands of garden-lovers, particularly between the end of April and the beginning of June. It possesses the largest collection

Bremer Landesmuseum (Focke-Museum)
Schwachhauser Heerstrasse 240, tel. (0421) 361-3575, fax (0241) 361-3903.
Opening times: Tuesday to Sunday, 10.00 am to 6.00 pm; closed on Monday.

Rhododendronpark: enchanting corners such as this one attract numerous visitors to the gardens even when there is no display of blossom.

of species and types of this botanical family in Europe; some of them are in the open air, some in greenhouses. The park also has an extensive azalea museum (only open to the public during the blossom season) and an enchanting botanical garden displaying the rich diversity of local plants and numerous others from foreign countries.

It also only takes 20 minutes on the bus to the Rennplatz (race-course), where flat races and steeplechases take place regularly between March and November. These events are attractive both to horse-lovers and to lovers of betting.

Azalea greenhouse in the Rhododendronpark.

Rhododendronpark and botanical garden:
Opening times: open parkland every day, 7.30 am until sunset.
Sortimentsgarten: *April to September, everyday, 7.30 am until sunset.*
Rhododendron houses: *Mon. to Fri., 10.00 am to 4.00 pm; Sat., 12.00 noon to 4.00 pm.*
Azalea Museum: *20th March to 30th April, as for Rhododendron houses.*

Industry in Bremen

Bremen's highly advanced industry profits considerably from the geographical advantage conferred by its seaport. Nowadays one job out of every three in the federal State of Bremen is still connected with the port industry, and the harbour (taking all activities together) is the biggest employer. Coffee may still be delivered in sacks, even these days, and cotton and tobacco in bales, all of which have to be unloaded - back-breaking manual work - but far more goods are now shipped in modern containers. Skilled workers can unload such a consignment in just a few hours (and they work round the clock), thanks to sophisticated modern technology and logistics; this saves there customers expensive demurrage charges. Many of these container ships were laid down in the wharves along the Weser such as Bremer Vulkan and the Lloyd wharf in Bremerhaven, which also supply special ships with highly technical equipment and elegant cruise liners. They are also becoming more and more involved in the fields of environmental and marine technology. A similar process of adaptation to the needs of the day has also been successfully completed by the Lürsen yard, in the Vegesack, which now specialises in luxury yachts.

Just as the harbour is in the business of bringing raw materials ashore, there is a closely related industry engaged in processing them. Thus half the coffee drunk in Germany comes from the roasting-houses in Bremen (Jacobs, Eduscho, Hag, and Melitta); the names of Suchard, Milka, and Haschez stand for chocolate products, and Kellogg's for Corn Flakes (based on maize). Tobacco, tea, and spices are also processed in Bremen, and in Bremerhaven they process the freshly landed fish. Bremen's best-known brewery, Beck's, profits from its position next to the harbour and exports a large proportion of its production.

The largest private-sector employer is Mercedes-Benz AG, which has been producing light trucks in Bremen since 1971 and now also assembles sports and saloon cars in the Sebaldsbrück district. As it also needs more than 1,000 firms to supply it with goods and services, this major company indirectly provides numerous other jobs in the region. The motor construction industry can look back on a fine tradition in Bremen, linked with the names of Hansa-Lloyd and Borgward; lovers of veteran cars still savour them with relish.

Even before this time, the engineers Focke and Wulf were building high-performance aircraft without knowing that they were thus laying the foundation stone for Bremen's present-day aerospace industry. The firm of Deutsche Aerospace produces the wings here for the modern Airbus airliner; they are then packed on board an enormous airfreighter and sent via Bremen's modern airport to Toulouse, in France, to be assembled onto the fuselages. The company also works on the development of space travel projects and produces parts for the European „Ariane" rocket.

This industry, and many more besides, are assisted by the University of Bremen and its many different organisations and institutes, which include futuristic and practical-minded research in the extensive technology park all round the university. Its hallmark is the 146-metre tall free-fall tower, in which weightlessness can be simulated for brief periods (4.7 seconds, at 167 k.p.h.) before the test vehicle is brought to a halt in a dense layer of styropor pellets. This is the only tower of its kind, and belongs to the „Centre for applied space travel technology and microgravitation" of the University of Bremen, which was also responsible for the development of the „BremSat" research satellite. This is now transmitting valuable data to Earth from its space orbit.

▲ Inspecting the quality of raw coffee beans.

▲ Brewing pan in a major brewery. ▼ Part of a car factory. ▲ Free-fall tower.

Unique to Bremen

There can hardly be any other major city in Germany in which traditional customs enjoy the same prestige as in Bremen. The event with the longest tradition behind it is **the Freimarkt,** of which there is documentary evidence dating back to 1035, making it the oldest Volksfest in Germany. During the only trade fair in the centre of the city,

Bremen's Roland colourfully decorated for the Freimarkt.

jugglers, singers, and actors entertained the numerous guests.

This developed over the centuries into a fairground which was established outside the old city centre in 1913. The attractions are set up nowadays mainly on the Bürgerweide, although some of them have now returned to the market square. This is where night-life is then concentrated, here and in the nearby taverns, during the two weeks of October, publicly supported by the temporary abolition of „closing time" all over Bremen, by cheap bus and tram tickets, and by a special night-time bus and tram service. Even the dignified figure of Roland blossoms forth in festive grandeur, decorated with coloured balloons and a gigantic heart-shaped spiced cake, the Lebkuchen beloved of autumn and Christmas fairs all over Germany.

Freimarkt: airborne excitement on the chair-o-plane.

He looks across towards the cathedral doorway under the North Tower, where the surprised visitor can sometimes watch an unusual ceremony called **„Domtreppenfegen"** - sweeping the cathedral steps. It is customary amongst the locals for anyone who is still unmarried on his 30th birthday to place an advertisement in the newspaper publicly inviting all his friends and relations to appear on that day in front of the cathedral. To the strains of a hurdy-gurdy he has to sweep up all the confetti scattered around; he can take a strengthening drink from time to time to keep himself going. Unmarried ladies are likewise not spared any punishment; they have to polish the door handle until they are released from further duty by a warm-hearted kiss.

A Bremen tradition: „Domtreppenfegen" in front of the door at the foot of the North Tower.

The **Schaffermahl** in the Upper Hall of the town hall is one of the grandest traditional events in Bremen. It dates back to 1525, and was once a farewell banquet at the end of the winter at which merchants, ship-owners, and ship's captains (it often happened that one person was all three at once) would discuss the business affairs for the coming season. The rules laid down in those days are still strictly adhered to: three selected merchants (the „Schaffer") paid the bill and thus acquired the right to attend the banquet in all subsequent years; prominent guests are allowed to attend once, women never. The menu is also laid down by tradition, and includes **Braunkohl mit Pinkel** (anyone who cannot guess what this might be should see the explanation below) and smoked meats, roast veal with plums, Riga

halibut, and stockfish. A special „seafarer's beer" also used to be brewed for the occasion. Another special feature is the sheets of blotting paper laid out for the guests to wipe their knives and forks on between courses, as was customary on board the cramped sailing ships.

Outsiders are also allowed to enjoy the „national dish of Bremen" heartily between January and March. Braunkohl is in fact green cabbage, and Pinkel is a highly seasoned sausage containing bacon, oats, and onions. During this season, walks and trips on dry land and by water are offered with the aim that the merry company and the exercise will help with the digestion of this hefty meal, with the additional help if necessary of a certain amount of the appropriate liquid.

Schaffermahl: a view across the decorated tables and the ceremonially dressed guests at the traditional banquet in the Upper Hall of the town hall.

The ingredients and trimmings for „Bremen's national dish" of „Braunkohl und Pinkel". „Kohlfahrten", outings during which these are eaten, have been a Bremen tradition for centuries.

This trips developed into a new tradition in 1829, called the **Eiswette**. Every year, on the first Sunday after Epiphany, dignified gentlemen dressed in frock coats and top hats meet by the Weser, accompanied by the Three Kings of the Epiphany, to find out whether a slender tailor's boy can cross the river dry-shod. As the Weser has not frozen over for several decades now, lots are cast to decide whether the „ice wager" has been won or lost; the loser pays for the dinner: Kohl und Pinkel as the main course, with warming drinks to accompany it. However, the real winner is the German Society for rescuing shipwrecked mariners, which is based in Bremen and receives a suitable donation from all concerned.

The „slender tailor" is one of the chief characters in the traditional „Eiswette".

Bremen-Vegesack

Vegesack may be on the northern fringes of Bremen, but it is one of its best-known suburbs. 17 kilometres downstream on the Weser, it can be reached most easily on the local passenger train, the Citybahn, which takes 20 minutes. The walk from the station to the harbour at the confluence of the Schönebecker Aue only takes a few minutes. After the lower Weser had silted up heavily in the 17th century, the city of Bremen founded its first „subsidiary" port here in 1619; it was the first artificial harbour anywhere in Germany. However, the process of silting progressed remorselessly, and Bremen first had to transfer its outport into Lower Saxony before, in 1823, the town was able to buy the land to build a new outport, „Bremer Hafen". In the meantime, however, ship's captains and pilots had built their retirement homes in Vegesack, and rows of uniform little houses with tidy front gardens gave this friendly harbour town the typical character it still has today. 18th century warehouses are still to be found in the port area, and are still in use, but mainly for cultural purposes. A reproduction of the jaw of a blue whale, 7.1 metres long and 1 metre thick, and its inscription, remind us of the days when sailing ships went out hunting whales, and a signpost showing the names of many ports all over the world remind us of the era of Vegesack's greatest importance.

Vegesack: a historical sailing ship in front of the port captain's house.

Information

KITO (a centre for cultural and other events): Opening times: Wednesday and Thursday, 11.00 am to 7.00 pm; Saturday and Sunday, 11.00 am to 6.00 pm. **Museum of local arts and crafts, Schloss Schönebeck:** *Im Dorfe 3-5, 28757 Bremen, tel.: (0421) 62 34 32. Opening times: Tuesday, Wednesday, and Saturday, 3.00 to 5.00 pm; Sunday, 10.00 am to 12.30 pm and 3.00 to 5.00 pm.*

Reproduction of the jaw of a blue whale, the hallmark of the harbour of Vegesack.

Shanty singer at the Vegesack harbour festival.

It is well worthwhile taking a walk from here along the Weser promenade to see ocean-going vessels passing only a short distance away from the onlooker, or a stroll through the pedestrian zone ending cosily in one of more than 50 hotels, restaurants, cafés, and taverns, which crowd especially close together in the port area. Exciting trips can be made by boat to the Frisian islands, to Heligoland, Bremerhaven, or just the short distance to the artists' village of Worpswede. You can also reach Schloss Schönebeck, in the valley of the Schönebecker Aue, by bus (route 78/79) or on foot; it is an unadorned brick-faced building with a double-sloping roof set in attractive parkland, and has been in the possession of the City of Bremen since 1952. It is made available nowadays to the Museum Association for its collections. In addition to exhibits reflecting the home lives of ordinary citizens, there are many pictures and exhibits commemorating the days of sailing ships and steamships, of fishing boats which brought back herring or even a whale, and of journeys by research ships to Greenland and Africa.

Worpswede: the Barkenhoff, once the residence of the artist Heinrich Vogeler, with its lively façade and outside staircase.

Excursions to the surrounding area

One of the most attractive destinations anywhere around Bremen is the world-famous artists' village of Worpswede, which can be reached in 45 minutes from the mainline station by bus route 140. Until about the end of the 19th century it was a farming village, living mainly from peat-cutting, but the attention of the artistic world was directed to it in 1895 by a joint exhibition by the Worpswede painters' association in Munich. At the instigation of Fritz Mackensen, he and his colleagues from student days, Otto

Modersohn and Hans, settled here in 1889, followed later by Fritz Overbeck and Heinrich Vogeler. They were most enthusiastic about the heavy landscape of the Teufelsmoor and the original populace; both were, for these artists, the quintessence of unspoiled naturalness. These landscape painters were followed by generations of young artists, and now the population here is made up not only of painters but also of sculptors, graphic artists, potters, weavers, composers, musicians, photographers, writers, goldsmiths, glass-blowers, and engravers. Bergstrasse starts just opposite the Hemberg bus-stop, and we can follow it a few yards to the central car-park. A footpath leads from here to the Café Worpswede, an idiosyncratic building designed by the sculptor and architect Bernhard Hoetger, who also created the neighbouring cultural centre which is well worth seeing. It contains the „grand show

Enchanting corner in the artists' village of Worpswede.

Hoetger sculpture in the park in front of the Café Worpswede, also known as „Café Verrückt" („Café Crazy").

of art" with exhibits by the best-known Worpswede artists, a „graphotek" with exhibits reflecting contemporary art, and, in the next-door building, the Ludwig Roselius Museum of early history; there are also numerous sculptures in the park. If we now follow the footpath parallel to Bergstrasse we will come out on Lindenallee. Turning left and walking another 15 minutes we come to the Niedersachsenstein, which is also a work by Hoetger, and the Philine-Vogeler-Haus just opposite the entrance to the park and serving nowadays as a tourist information office. From here, the nearby spire will lead us up to the 18th-century church of Zion, and inside this we can

learn a nice little story about the young artists Clara Westhoff and Paula Becker-Modersohn. On 12th August 1900, in a fit of daring, she rang the church bell and thus called the fire brigade out on full alert. By way of punishment she had to redesign the interior of the church artistically. Her and Clara's production and ornamentation are to this day the only decoration in this plain church. Paula, after marrying Otto Modersohn, died as early as 1907 shortly after the birth of her first child. Her grave, near the new cemetery chapel, was designed by Bernhard Hoetger and thus pays homage to an artist who nowadays enjoys the highest level of awareness of all the Worpswede masters.

Findorffstrasse, below the church, and the nearby monument as well, commemorate the „royal marsh commissar" Christian Finndorff, later lovingly known as the „father of the marsh". He had arranged for the church to be built, the tower of which is now a landmark visible from far and wide. The street that branches off from it, "Bauernreihe", leads us to a number of typical peatcutters' houses, some of them still reed-

All exhibitions in Worpswede: *daily 10.00 am to 6.00 pm.*

Information

A view of unspoilt Nature on the Teufelsmoor.

Two shorter route lead in a huge curve starting from below the church; No. 1, 2.5 kilometres long, goes past the Findorff memorial and over the Weyerberg (54 metres high, with a fine view) to the Niedersachsenstein and then back via Lindenallee. No. 2 (4.5 kilometres) leads all round the Weyerberg.

Another possible way of exploring the village is simple to stroll through its streets. The pleasing houses mainly hide behind park-like front gardens. There is a strikingly large number of art galleries, studios, boutiques, and exhibition and sale rooms for arts and crafts of all kinds. Visitors are free to browse around as much as they like. The particularly interesting buildings here are the Barkenhoff, which belonged to Heinrich Vogeler and is now the home of the Barkenhoff Foundation for encouraging young artists as well as an exhibition room, and the "Haus im Schluh", where the successors of Heinrich Vogeler now work and exhibit. Anyone who wanders through the street of Worpswede with only half an eye open will gain an impression of the significance of this artists' colony right up to the present day. There has been a second such colony in Fischerhude, about 20 kilometres east of Bremen in the Wümme valley, since about 1900, and this has been able to retain its rural character even more than its famous sister-village.

thatched, with plain brick-faced or half-timbered façades. Some of the drainage channels on the Hammeniederung side have still been preserved, as are the romantic windmills. On the far side of the railway line, hiking and cycling route lead out onto Teufelsmoor, where the visit can discover unspoiled spots in the Breites Wasser nature conservancy area and elsewhere in this wide, marshy landscape.

Typical farmhouse in Fischerhude.

Bremerhaven

As the name alone indicates, Bremerhaven belongs to Bremen, 65 kilometres away, but it is still a city in its own right with 130,000 inhabitants and the only one, apart from Bremen itself, in the present-day federal state of the „Free Hanseatic City of Bremen". Within the state it is dependent on Bremen, the mayor of which is at the same time the called Alter Hafen, was finished in 1830, and after that there was no stopping the upward climb of the newly established city. Hanover then founded the port of Geestemünde in the immediate vicinity by way of competition, and it soon gained considerable significance on account of its high seas fishing fleet and its shipbuilding yards. Under Prussian rule, Geestemünde was united with Lehe to its north to form the town of

Aerial view of part of the Bremerhaven port area. The locks leading into the fishing port and the Seebeckwerft can be seen, as well as the radar tower and, on the left of it, the prominent building of the Alfred-Wegener-Institut.

Minister-President of the State. Bremerhaven owes its existence to the mayor of Bremen of the day, Johann Smidt, as he bought a strip of land totalling 89 hectares (220 acres) from the Kingdom of Hanover, as it then was, in 1827; this land is now the centre of the city and the port area. Establishing this harbour solved two problems at once for Smidt: the silting up of the Weser and the customs duties demanded by the states along its banks. The first basin, now Wesermünde, which at the same time encircled Bremerhaven like a clamp and threatened to strangle it.

In 1939, the town of Wesermünde was integrated into Bremerhaven, leaving only the overseas harbour in the possession of the city of Bremen. After the second world war, American occupation forces took over the city (or as much as was still standing - warfare had destroyed 97% of it) and the port area. The present political geography was

German Maritime Museum: Figurehead and illumination of a lighthouse.

created in 1949, with Wesermünde and Bremerhaven forming part of the federal State of Bremen, to which the fishing ports belong. The overseas port is still in the possession of the City of Bremen. Because the history of the development of Bremerhaven is relatively short, the sights to see in the city are limited to only two centuries. Like the city itself, they relate mainly to the sea and seafaring. The main point of attraction is in the area of the Alter Hafen (1827-1830), which used to be joined by a lock to the Lesum but this has now been filled in. The German Maritime Museum has been housed here since 1975. In the harbour basin there are such interesting vessels as the Seute Deern, and wooden-hulled full-masted ship dating from 1919, the Grönland, which travelled with the first German polar expedition in 1868, the Elbe 3, a fire-fighting ship built in 1909 and still in service up to 1966, the Ran IX, a steam-driven whaler built in 1939 later used to hunt submarines and clear mines, and a U-boat, the Wilhelm Bauer, which can now be visited as a floating museum. There are in total more than 100 original vessels on this site, including a Bremen Hanseatic „Kogge" dating from 1380 and a large number of models, parts of ships, pictures, and mementoes of seafaring days.

The best way of looking all across the museum site, the city, and the port area is from the viewing platform of the radar tower, which is 112 metres tall to the top of its aerial. From the estuary of the Geeste, a 100-metre long double lock leads to the two fishing harbours which are amongst the biggest in Europe, covering 700 hectares (1,700 acres). Not only the smaller fishing boats but also enormous fishery factory ships land their catches here from all parts of the world's oceans. Fish processing factories, fish auction sheds, refrigerated stores, and even a fish restaurant huddle together into the harbour

Fish auction in one of the three huge auction-halls.

German Maritime Museum:
Opening times: Tuesday ot Sunday, 10.00 am to 6.00 pm, closed on Mondays, tel. (0471) 482070

district, which is dominated by the old lighthouse of Brinkamahof. It is also possible to enjoy a fine view of the fishing harbour from its platform, and over the old trade harbour, now occupied by a shipyard. Like the fishing harbours, the trade harbour is linked by a freight station to the German railway network. On the west bank of the trade harbour stands a striking building like a ship's bow; this is the Alfred-Wegener-Institut for maritime research. Its exhibition shows a representative cross-section of all forms of life in the salt water of the North Sea: mammals, sea birds, reptiles, fishes, crabs, mussels, sponges, corals, and plants.

Downstream on the Weser, the Alter Hafen is adjoined by the Neuer Hafen (1847-52), nowadays reserved for water-sports and inland sailors. Between the Neuer Hafen and the Weser is a public hall, the Strandhalle, and the Tiergrotten, also called the „zoo by the

Historic brick lighthouse in the old tug harbour.

Seals in the „Tiergrotten", the Bremerhaven zoo.

sea", which houses mainly the Nordic species of animals but also a „howling station" for orphaned seal-cubs and large aquaria containing all the species of fish in the North Sea. On the other side of the filled-in lock, the romantic old lighthouse (1857, 37 metres tall) still acts as a steering mark for seagoing ships.

Behind the next bridge is Kaiserhafen I,

mainly a naval base today, and then numbers II and III (1906-09) with their huge warehouses. These latter two are part of the customs-free area of the overseas harbour, which has parking space for 80,000 cars and is Europe's largest landing port for the import and export of motor vehicles being shipped between the continent of Europe, Great Britain, the USA, and south-east Asia. The three Kaiserhafen docks were connected with the open sea by the Kaiserschleuse, a lock built in 1897 and, with a length of 222 metres and a width of 45 metres was the biggest in the world for a time. Through it, sea-going ships travel through outer dock into the enormous Kaiserdock of the Lloyd shipyard with its modern fruit terminal, which is the leading one in Germany particularly for the transhipment of bananas.

Beyond the fruit terminal, the outer dock and the north lock (1931) lead into the gigantic Nordhafen and Osthafen, together with their extensive winding basins. The lock alone is 372 metres long and 60 metres wide, making it still one of the largest in the world. Beyond it, the City of Bremerhaven has built Europe's largest container transhipment installations, called the Wilhelm Kaisen Container Terminal. The container ships mainly moor up against the Stromkaje, 3.2 kilometres long, directly on the Weser, and are loaded or unloaded in record time by the numerous container cranes.

However, this outport of Bremen is in the lead not only in respect of freight transport. Between the two huge locks along the Weser lies the famous Columbuskaje, once the mooring for numerous ships carrying emigrants to America. Passenger ships still depart regularly from here for cruises and excursions to Heligoland. Whilst part of the quay is taken up by the modern passenger-handling hall, the other has been converted into a terminal for mixed cargoes. The world's biggest rotating bridge spans the waterway between the Verbindungshafen and the Osthafen and enables passengers and goods to reach the Columbuskaje. It can also be reached by pedestrians walking from the maritime museum along Deichpromenade.

Away to one side of the harbour district, a statue in front of the municipal theatre commemorates Mayor Smidt, the founder of Bremerhaven. Alongside the theatre are the neatly tended Bürgerpark and the Speckenbüttel open-air museum, which offers a row of local farm houses dating from the 16th century onwards, all carefully dismantled, brought to this site, reconstructed, and restored.

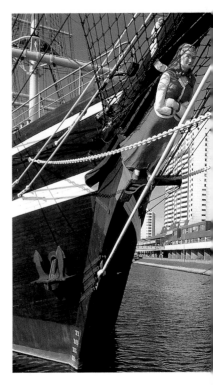

Snap-shots of life in Bremerhaven's busy port.

Emigrants' memorial.

Tips and addresses from A to Z

Airport: Airport information, tel. 55951

Buses and trams:
Customer service no.: 5596-333

Camping: Campingplatz Bremen, tel. 212002

Car service:
ADAC breakdown service, tel. 01802/222222

Casino: Böttcherstrasse 3, opening times:
Sunday to Thursday, 3.00 pm to 2.00 am;
Friday and Saturday, 3.00 pm to 3.00 am,
tel. 329000

Cinemas (selected): City Filmtheater, tel. 13757;
Europa-Filmpalast, tel. 13663; Vereinigte Filmtheater GmbH, tel. 12982

Congress-Centrum:
Hollerallee 99, tel. 3789-0, Fax 3789600

Currency exchange: Postamt 5 (with Post
Office savings bank counter), Bahnhofsplatz
21, Monday to Friday, 8.00 am to 6.00 pm;
Saturday, 8.00 am to 1.00 pm; Sunday, 9.00
to 10.00 am. Currency exchange inside
mainline railway station - Deutsche Verkehrs-
und Kreditbank: Monday to Friday, 7.30 am
to 7.00 pm; Saturday, 8.00 am to 12.00
noon and 1.00 to 4.00 pm. Airport - Deutsche Bank: Monday to Friday, 1.00 to 8.00
pm (not continuously), Saturday 9.00 am to
2.00 pm

Guided tours of Bremen: Historical town
centre, every day at 2.00 pm, starting from
the Tourist Information Office at the mainline
station, duration: 1½ to 2 hours

Information: Tourist Offices, mainline station
and Liebfrauen Kirchhof: Monday to Wednesday and Friday, 9.30 am to 6.30 pm; Thursday, 9.30 am to 8.30 pm; Saturday, 9.30 am
to 2.00 pm; Sunday, 9.30 am to 3.30 pm

Opera/Operetta: Theater am Goetheplatz,
tel. 36530; Congress Centre, tel. 37890

Post Office, Telegrams: Bahnhofsplatz 21,
every day from 7.00 am to 10.00 pm

Rail services (mainline): tel. 19419

Shipping lines: Helgoland services, tel. 04464/
8021; Schreiner, tel. 321229; Halover, tel. 74859

Sightseeing bus tours: Every day at 10.30 am,
starting from the main bus station in front of the
mainline railway station. Duration: 2 hours

Special envents: Information and reservations:
Tourist office (Verkehrsverein), tel. 30800-0
or Ticket Service Centre, tel. 358293

Sports facilities: Football: Weser Stadion,
tel. 434500; Horse-racing, tel. 463307;
Bowling: Bowl'n Fun, tel. 3365530; Ten-pin
bowling: Findorff, tel. 351005; Kegelzentrum:
tel. 513338

Swimming facilities (selected):
Indoor: Aquadrom, tel. 427470; Huchting,
tel. 580083; Piaskowski, tel. 662240; Out-
door: Horner Bad, Tel. 237577; Heidbergbad,
tel. 631637; Waller See-Bad, tel. 612372

Taxis: Taxi-Roland, tel. 14433;
Taxi-Ruf, tel. 14014; Auto-Engel, tel. 504151

Theatres (selected):
Theater am Goetheplatz, Schauspielhaus, and
Concordia have the following telephone num-
bers: central exchange 36530, box office
3653333, Monday to Friday 1.00 to 6.00 pm,
Saturday 11.00 am to 2.00 pm. Ernst Waldau
Theater, tel. 383031; Theater im Schnoor, tel.
326054

Tourist Office: Hillmannplatz 6, 28195 Bre-
men, tel. 0421/30800-0, fax 30800-30;
Monday to Thursday, 9.00 am to 4.00 pm;
Friday 9.00 am to 2.00 pm

Variety theatre:
Transvestiten Theater Madame Lothar,
Kolpingstrasse 9 (Schnoor), tel. 3379191

Youth Hostel:
Bremen Youth Hostel, tel. 171369;
Worpswede Youth Hostel, tel. 04792/360